Briathra

A Student's
Guide to
Irish Verbs

Eoghan Beglan

Clár

Na Briathra Neamhrialta

The Irregular Verbs

Briathra Eile 101

Other Verbs

Réamhfhocail 103

Prepositions

Cleachtadh na mBriathra 107

Practise the Verbs

Réamhrá

Introduction

The verbs in this book are divided into two main sections:

1. Briathra Rialta Comónta – Common Regular Verbs.

Regular Verbs are divided into two sections: **An Chéad Réimniú** – *The First Conjugation* (verbs containing just one syllable) and **An Dara Réimniú** – *The Second Conjugation* (verbs containing two syllables).

2. Na Briathra Neamhrialta – *The Irregular Verbs* – there are just 11 of these.

Each colour coded verb is conjugated in the *Aimsir Chaite*, *Aimsir Láithreach*, *Aimsir Fháistineach* and in the **Modh Coinníollach**, along with the **Modh Ceisteach**, which will help you to ask and answer questions in each tense.

To further aid you in your learning, this book includes:

– A **Briathra Eile** (*Other Verbs*) section that opens up a wider range of verbs that share similar endings.

– A useful **Réamhfhocail** (*Prepositions*) section which helps you to form and connect phrases in your sentences (e.g. Rith an madra **chugam**).

– A **Cleachtadh na mBriathra** (*Practice the Verbs*) template which can be photocopied for use in your exercises.

The terms *slender* and *broad* refer to two categories of vowels: the broad vowels (a, o and u) and the slender vowels (e and i). When writing verbs, we make sure that the vowels on either side of a consonant (or group of consonants) agree – in other words, they should both be broad vowels or both be slender vowels.

Bris
to break

Aimsir Chaite	Aimsir Láithreach
Bhris mé	Bris**im**
Bhris tú	Bris**eann** tú
Bhris sé	Bris**eann** sé
Bhris sí	Bris**eann** sí
Bhris**eamar**	Bris**imid**
Bhris sibh	Bris**eann** sibh
Bhris siad	Bris**eann** siad
Ar bhris?	**An mb**riseann?
✓ **Bh**ris	✓ Bris**eann**
✓ **Níor bh**ris	✗ **Ní bh**riseann

Aimsir Fháistineach	Modh Coinníollach
Bris**fidh** mé	**Bhris**finn
Bris**fidh** tú	**Bhris**feá
Bris**fidh** sé	**Bhris**feadh sé
Bris**fidh** sí	**Bhris**feadh sí
Bris**fimid**	**Bhris**fimis
Bris**fidh** sibh	**Bhris**feadh sibh
Bris**fidh** siad	**Bhris**fidís
An mbris**fidh**?	**An mb**ris**feadh**?
✓ Bris**fidh**	✓ **Bhris**feá
✗ **Ní bh**ris**fidh**	✗ **Ní bhris**feadh

Buaigh
to win

Aimsir Chaite	Aimsir Láithreach
Bhuaigh mé	Bu**aim**
Bhuaigh tú	Bu**ann** tú
Bhuaigh sé	Bu**ann** sé
Bhuaigh sí	Bu**ann** sí
Bhuamar	Bu**aimid**
Bhuaigh sibh	Bu**ann** sibh
Bhuaigh siad	Bu**ann** siad
Ar bhuaigh?	**An mb**uann?
✓ **Bh**uaigh	✓ Bu**ann**
✗ **Níor bh**uaigh	✗ **Ní bh**uann

Aimsir Fháistineach	Modh Coinníollach
Bua**faidh** mé	**Bh**uafainn
Bua**faidh** tú	**Bh**uafá
Bua**faidh** sé	**Bh**ua**fadh** sé
Bua**faidh** sí	**Bh**ua**fadh** sí
Bua**faimid**	**Bh**ua**faimis**
Bua**faidh** sibh	**Bh**ua**fadh** sibh
Bua**faidh** siad	**Bh**ua**faidís**

An mbua**faidh**?	**An mb**ua**fadh**?
✓ Bua**faidh**	✓ **Bh**ua**fadh**
✗ **Ní bh**ua**faidh**	✗ **Ní bh**ua**fadh**

Caill

to lose

Aimsir Chaite	Aimsir Láithreach
Chaill mé	Caill**im**
Chaill tú	Caill**eann** tú
Chaill sé	Caill**eann** sé
Chaill sí	Caill**eann** sí
Chaill**eamar**	Caill**imid**
Chaill sibh	Caill**eann** sibh
Chaill siad	Caill**eann** siad

Ar chaill?	**An gc**aill**eann**?
✓ **Ch**aill	✓ Caill**eann**
✗ **Níor** chaill	✗ **Ní ch**aill**eann**

7

Aimsir Fháistineach	Modh Coinníollach
Caill**fidh** mé	**Ch**aill**finn**
Caill**fidh** tú	**Ch**aill**feá**
Caill**fidh** sé	**Ch**aill**feadh** sé
Caill**fidh** sí	**Ch**aill**feadh** sí
Caill**fimid**	**Ch**aill**fimis**
Caill**fidh** sibh	**Ch**aill**feadh** sibh
Caill**fidh** siad	**Ch**aill**fidís**
An gcaill**fidh**?	**An gc**aill**feadh**?
✓ Caill**fidh**	✓ **Ch**aill**feadh**
✗ **Ní ch**aill**fidh**	✗ **Ní ch**aill**feadh**

Caith

to throw / to spend / to wear

slender

Aimsir Chaite

Chaith mé

Chaith tú

Chaith sé

Chaith sí

Chaith**eamar**

Chaith sibh

Chaith siad

Ar **ch**aith?

✓ **Ch**aith

✗ **Níor ch**aith

Aimsir Láithreach

Caith**im**

Ca**ith**eann tú

Ca**ith**eann sé

Ca**ith**eann sí

Caith**imid**

Ca**ith**eann sibh

Ca**ith**eann siad

An gcaith**eann**?

✓ Caith**eann**

✗ **Ní ch**aith**eann**

Aimsir Fháistineach

Caith**fidh** mé ← *Also means* '*I must…*'

Caith**fidh** tú

Caith**fidh** sé

Caith**fidh** sí

Caith**fimid**

Caith**fidh** sibh

Caith**fidh** siad

An gcaith**fidh**?

✓ Caith**fidh**

✗ **Ní ch**aith**fidh**

Modh Coinníollach

Chaith**finn**

Chaith**feá**

Chaith**feadh** sé

Chaith**feadh** sí

Chaith**fimis**

Chaith**feadh** sibh

Chaith**fidís**

An gcaith**feadh**?

✓ **Ch**aith**feadh**

✗ **Ní ch**aith**feadh**

Cuir
to put

Aimsir Chaite	Aimsir Láithreach
Chuir mé	Cuir**im**
Chuir tú	Cuir**eann** tú
Chuir sé	Cuir**eann** sé
Chuir sí	Cuir**eann** sí
Chuir**eamar**	Cuir**imid**
Chuir sibh	Cuir**eann** sibh
Chuir siad	Cuir**eann** siad
Ar chuir?	**An g**cuir**eann**?
✓ **Ch**uir	✓ Cuir**eann**
✗ **Níor ch**uir	✗ **Ní ch**uir**eann**

Aimsir Fháistineach	Modh Coinníollach
Cui**rfidh** mé	**Chuirfinn**
Cui**rfidh** tú	**Chuirfeá**
Cui**rfidh** sé	**Chuirfeadh** sé
Cui**rfidh** sí	**Chuirfeadh** sí
Cui**rfimid**	**Chuirfimis**
Cui**rfidh** sibh	**Chuirfeadh** sibh
Cui**rfidh** siad	**Chuirfidís**
An gcui**rfidh**?	**An g**cui**rfeadh**?
✓ Cui**rfidh**	✓ **Chuirfeadh**
✗ **Ní ch**ui**rfidh**	✗ **Ní chuirfeadh**

Díol
to sell

Aimsir Chaite	Aimsir Láithreach
Dhíol mé	Díol**aim**
Dhíol tú	Díol**ann** tú
Dhíol sé	Díol**ann** sé
Dhíol sí	Díol**ann** sí
Dhíolamar	Díol**aimid**
Dhíol sibh	Díol**ann** sibh
Dhíol siad	Díol**ann** siad

Ar dhíol?	**An nd**íol**ann**?
✓ **Dh**íol	✓ Díol**ann**
✗ **Níor dh**íol	✗ **Ní dh**íol**ann**

Aimsir Fháistineach	Modh Coinníollach
Díol**faidh** mé	**Dh**íol**fainn**
Díol**faidh** tú	**Dh**íol**fá**
Díol**faidh** sé	**Dh**íol**fadh** sé
Díol**faidh** sí	**Dh**íol**fadh** sí
Díol**faimid**	**Dh**íol**faimis**
Díol**faidh** sibh	**Dh**íol**fadh** sibh
Díol**faidh** siad	**Dh**íol**faidís**
An ndíol**faidh**?	**An n**díol**fadh**?
✓ Díol**faidh**	✓ **Dh**íol**fadh**
✗ **Ní dh**íol**faidh**	✗ **Ní dh**íol**fadh**

Dóigh
to burn

Aimsir Chaite	Aimsir Láithreach
Dhóigh mé	Dó**im**
Dhóigh tú	Dó**nn** tú
Dhóigh sé	Dó**nn** sé
Dhóigh sí	Dó**nn** sí
Dhómar	Dó**imid**
Dhóigh sibh	Dó**nn** sibh
Dhóigh siad	Dó**nn** siad
Ar dh**óigh?**	**An ndón**n?
✓ **Dh**óigh	✓ Dó**nn**
✗ **Níor** dhóigh	✗ **Ní dh**ónn

Aimsir Fháistineach	Modh Coinníollach
Dófaidh mé	Dhófainn
Dófaidh tú	Dhófá
Dófaidh sé	Dhófadh sé
Dófaidh sí	Dhófadh sí
Dófaimid	Dhófaimis
Dófaidh sibh	Dhófadh sibh
Dófaidh siad	Dhófaidís
An ndófaidh?	An ndófadh?
✓ Dófaidh	✓ Dhófadh
✗ Ní dhófaidh	✗ Ní dhófadh

Dún
to close

Aimsir Chaite	Aimsir Láithreach
Dhún mé	Dún**aim**
Dhún tú	Dún**ann** tú
Dhún sé	Dún**ann** sé
Dhún sí	Dún**ann** sí
Dhún**amar**	Dún**aimid**
Dhún sibh	Dún**ann** sibh
Dhún siad	Dún**ann** siad

Ar dhún?	**An nd**ún**ann**?
✓ **Dh**ún	✓ Dún**ann**
✗ **Níor dh**ún	✗ **Ní dh**ún**ann**

Aimsir Fháistineach	Modh Coinníollach
Dúnfaidh mé	Dhúnfainn
Dúnfaidh tú	Dhúnfá
Dúnfaidh sé	Dhúnfadh sé
Dúnfaidh sí	Dhúnfadh sí
Dúnfaimid	Dhúnfaimis
Dúnfaidh sibh	Dhúnfadh sibh
Dúnfaidh siad	Dhúnfaidís

An ndúnfaidh?	**An ndúnfadh?**
✓ Dúnfaidh	✓ Dhúnfadh
✗ Ní dhúnfaidh	✗ Ní dhúnfadh

Fan
to wait

Aimsir Chaite

D'fhan mé

D'fhan tú

D'fhan sé

D'fhan sí

D'fhanamar

D'fhan sibh

D'fhan siad

Ar fhan?

✓ **D'f**han

✗ **Níor fhan**

Aimsir Láithreach

Fan**aim**

Fan**ann** tú

Fan**ann** sé

Fan**ann** sí

Fan**aimid**

Fan**ann** sibh

Fan**ann** siad

An bhfan**ann**?

✓ Fan**ann**

✗ **Ní fhanann**

Aimsir Fháistineach	Modh Coinníollach
Fan**faidh** mé	**D'**fhan**fainn**
Fan**faidh** tú	**D'**fhan**fá**
Fan**faidh** sé	**D'**fhan**fadh** sé
Fan**faidh** sí	**D'**fhan**fadh** sí
Fan**faimid**	**D'**fhan**faimis**
Fan**faidh** sibh	**D'**fhan**fadh** sibh
Fan**faidh** siad	**D'**fhan**faidís**

An bhfanfaidh?	**An bhfanfadh?**
✓ Fan**faidh**	✓ **D'**fhan**fadh**
✗ **Ní fhanfaidh**	✗ **Ní fhanfadh**

Fág
to leave

Aimsir Chaite	Aimsir Láithreach
D'fhág mé	Fág**aim**
D'fhág tú	Fág**ann** tú
D'fhág sé	Fág**ann** sé
D'fhág sí	Fág**ann** sí
D'fhág**amar**	Fág**aimid**
D'fhág sibh	Fág**ann** sibh
D'fhág siad	Fág**ann** siad

Ar fhág?	**An bh**fág**ann**?
✓ **D'**fhág	✓ Fág**ann**
✗ **Níor** fhág	✗ **Ní fh**ág**ann**

Fág anseo é.

<table>
<tr><th>Aimsir Fháistineach</th><th>Modh Coinníollach</th></tr>
<tr><td>Fágfaidh mé</td><td>D'fhágfainn</td></tr>
<tr><td>Fágfaidh tú</td><td>D'fhágfá</td></tr>
<tr><td>Fágfaidh sé</td><td>D'fhágfadh sé</td></tr>
<tr><td>Fágfaidh sí</td><td>D'fhágfadh sí</td></tr>
<tr><td>Fágfaimid</td><td>D'fhágfaimis</td></tr>
<tr><td>Fágfaidh sibh</td><td>D'fhágfadh sibh</td></tr>
<tr><td>Fágfaidh siad</td><td>D'fhágfaidís</td></tr>
</table>

Aimsir Fháistineach	Modh Coinníollach
An bhfág**faidh**?	**An bh**fág**fadh**?
✓ Fág**faidh**	✓ **D'fhág**fadh
✗ **Ní fh**ág**faidh**	✗ **Ní fh**ág**fadh**

Féach
to look / to watch

Aimsir Chaite	Aimsir Láithreach
D'fhéach mé	Féach**aim**
D'fhéach tú	Féach**ann** tú
D'fhéach sé	Féach**ann** sé
D'fhéach sí	Féach**ann** sí
D'fhéach**amar**	Féach**aimid**
D'fhéach sibh	Féach**ann** sibh
D'fhéach siad	Féach**ann** siad

Ar fhéach?	**An bh**féac**ann**?
✓ **D'fh**éach	✓ Féach**ann**
✗ **Níor fh**éach	✗ **Ní fh**éach**ann**

Aimsir Fháistineach	Modh Coinníollach
Féach**faidh** mé	**D'fh**éach**fainn**
Féach**faidh** tú	**D'fh**éach**fá**
Féach**faidh** sé	**D'fh**éach**fadh** sé
Féach**faidh** sí	**D'fh**éach**fadh** sí
Féach**faimid**	**D'fh**éach**faimis**
Féach**faidh** sibh	**D'fh**éach**fadh** sibh
Féach**faidh** siad	**D'fh**éach**faidís**

An bhféach**faidh**?

✓ Féach**faidh**

✗ **Ní fh**éach**faidh**

An bhféach**fadh**?

✓ **D'fh**éach**fadh**

✗ **Ní fh**éach**fadh**

Gearr
to cut

Aimsir Chaite

Ghearr mé

Ghearr tú

Ghearr sé

Ghearr sí

Ghearr**amar**

Ghearr sibh

Ghearr siad

Ar ghearr?

✓ **Gh**earr

✗ **Níor gh**earr

Aimsir Láithreach

Gearr**aim**

Gearr**ann** tú

Gearr**ann** sé

Gearr**ann** sí

Gearr**aimid**

Gearr**ann** sibh

Gearr**ann** siad

An ngearr**ann**?

✓ Gearr**ann**

✗ **Ní gh**earr**ann**

Aimsir Fháistineach	Modh Coinníollach
Gearr**faidh** mé	**Ghearr**fainn
Gearr**faidh** tú	**Ghearr**fá
Gearr**faidh** sé	**Ghearr**fadh sé
Gearr**faidh** sí	**Ghearr**fadh sí
Gearr**faimid**	**Ghearr**faimis
Gearr**faidh** sibh	**Ghearr**fadh sibh
Gearr**faidh** siad	**Ghearr**fadh siad
An ngearr**faidh**?	**An ng**earr**fadh**?
✓ Gearr**faidh**	✓ **Ghearr**fadh
✗ **Ní gh**earr**faidh**	✗ **Ní gh**earr**fadh**

Glan
to clean

Aimsir Chaite	Aimsir Láithreach
Ghlan mé	Glan**aim**
Ghlan tú	Glan**ann** tú
Ghlan sé	Glan**ann** sé
Ghlan sí	Glan**ann** sí
Ghlan**amar**	Glan**aimid**
Ghlan sibh	Glan**ann** sibh
Ghlan siad	Glan**ann** siad
Ar ghlan?	**An ng**lan**ann**?
✓ **Gh**lan	✓ Glan**ann**
✗ **Níor gh**lan	✗ **Ní gh**lan**ann**

Aimsir Fháistineach	Modh Coinníollach
Glan**faidh** mé	**Gh**lan**fainn**
Glan**faidh** tú	**Gh**lan**fá**
Glan**faidh** sé	**Gh**lan**fadh** sé
Glan**faidh** sí	**Gh**lan**fadh** sí
Glan**faimid**	**Gh**lan**faimis**
Glan**faidh** sibh	**Gh**lan**fadh** sibh
Glan**faidh** siad	**Gh**lan**faidís**

An nglan**faidh**?	**An ng**lanfadh?
✓ Glan**faidh**	✓ **Gh**lanfadh
✗ **Ní gh**lan**faidh**	✗ **Ní gh**lanfadh

Léigh
to read

slender

Aimsir Chaite

Léigh mé

Léigh tú

Léigh sé

Léigh sí

Lé**amar**

Léigh sibh

Léigh siad

Ar léigh?

✓ Léigh

✗ **Níor** léigh

Aimsir Láithreach

Lé**im**

Lé**ann** tú

Lé**ann** sé

Lé**ann** sí

Lé**imid**

Lé**ann** sibh

Lé**ann** siad

An léann?

✓ Léann

✗ **Ní** léann

Aimsir Fháistineach	Modh Coinníollach
Léi**fidh** mé	Léi**finn**
Léi**fidh** tú	Léi**feá**
Léi**fidh** sé	Léi**feadh** sé
Léi**fidh** sí	Léi**feadh** sí
Léi**fimid**	Léi**fimis**
Léi**fidh** sibh	Léi**feadh** sibh
Léi**fidh** siad	Léi**fidís**

An léi**fidh**?	**An** léi**feadh**?
✓ Léi**fidh**	✓ Léi**feadh**
✗ **Ní** léi**fidh**	✗ **Ní** léi**feadh**

Líon
to fill

Aimsir Chaite

Líon mé

Líon tú

Líon sé

Líon sí

Líon**amar**

Líon sibh

Líon siad

Ar líon?

✓ Líon

✗ **Níor** líon

Aimsir Láithreach

Líon**aim**

Líon**ann** tú

Líon**ann** sé

Líon**ann** sí

Líon**aimid**

Líon**ann** sibh

Líon**ann** siad

An líon**ann**?

✓ Líon**ann**

✗ **Ní** líon**ann**

Aimsir Fháistineach	Modh Coinníollach
Líon**faidh** mé	Líon**fainn**
Líon**faidh** tú	Líon**fá**
Líon**faidh** sé	Líon**fadh** sé
Líon**faidh** sí	Líon**fadh** sí
Líon**faimid**	Líon**faimis**
Líon**faidh** sibh	Líon**fadh** sibh
Líon**faidh** siad	Líon**faidís**
An líon**faidh**?	**An** líon**fadh**?
✓ Líon**faidh**	✓ Líon**fadh**
✗ **Ní** líon**faidh**	✗ **Ní** líon**fadh**

Nigh
to wash

slender

Aimsir Chaite

Nigh mé

Nigh tú

Nigh sé

Nigh sí

Níomar

Nigh sibh

Nigh siad

Ar nigh?

✓ Nigh

✗ **Níor** nigh

Aimsir Láithreach

Ním

Níonn tú

Níonn sé

Níonn sí

Nímid

Níonn sibh

Níonn siad

An níonn?

✓ **Níonn**

✗ **Ní** níonn

Aimsir Fháistineach	Modh Coinníollach
Nífidh mé	Nífinn
Nífidh tú	Nífeá
Nífidh sé	Nífeadh sé
Nífidh sí	Nífeadh sí
Nífimid	Nífimis
Nífidh sibh	Nífeadh sibh
Nífidh siad	Nífidís
An nífidh?	An nífeadh?
✓ Nífidh	✓ Nífeadh
✗ Ní nífidh	✗ Ní nífeadh

Ól

to drink

Aimsir Chaite	Aimsir Láithreach
D'ól mé	**Ól**aim
D'ól tú	Ólann tú
D'ól sé	Ólann sé
D'ól sí	Ólann sí
D'ól**amar**	**Ól**aimid
D'ól sibh	Ólann sibh
D'ól siad	Ólann siad

Ar ól?	**An** ólann?
✓ **D'**ól	✓ Ólann
✗ **Níor** ól	✗ **Ní** ólann

35

Aimsir Fháistineach

Ólfaidh mé

Ólfaidh tú

Ólfaidh sé

Ólfaidh sí

Ólfaimid

Ólfaidh sibh

Ólfaidh siad

An ól**faidh**?

✓ **Ól**faidh

✗ **Ní** ól**faidh**

Modh Coinníollach

D'ólfainn

D'ólfá

D'ólfadh sé

D'ólfadh sí

D'ólfaimis

D'ólfadh sibh

D'ólfaidís

An ól**fadh**?

✓ **D'ól**fadh

✗ **Ní** ól**fadh**

Rith

to run

Aimsir Chaite

Rith mé

Rith tú

Rith sé

Rith sí

Rith**eamar**

Rith sibh

Rith siad

Ar rith?

✓ Rith

✗ **Níor** rith

Aimsir Láithreach

Rith**im**

Rith**eann** tú

Rith**eann** sé

Rith**eann** sí

Rith**imid**

Rith**eann** sibh

Rith**eann** siad

An ritheann?

✓ Rith**eann**

✗ **Ní** ritheann

Aimsir Fháistineach	Modh Coinníollach
Rith**fidh** mé	Rith**finn**
Rith**fidh** tú	Rith**feá**
Rith**fidh** sé	Rith**feadh** sé
Rith**fidh** sí	Rith**feadh** sí
Rith**fimid**	Rith**fimis**
Rith**fidh** sibh	Rith**feadh** sibh
Rith**fidh** siad	Rith**fidís**
An rith**fidh**?	**An** rith**feadh**?
✓ Rith**fidh**	✓ Rith**feadh**
✗ **Ní** rith**fidh**	✗ **Ní** rith**feadh**

Scríobh
to write

Aimsir Chaite

Scríobh mé

Scríobh tú

Scríobh sé

Scríobh sí

Scríobh**amar**

Scríobh sibh

Scríobh siad

Ar scríobh?

✓ Scríobh

✗ **Níor** scríobh

Aimsir Láithreach

Scríobh**aim**

Scríobh**ann** tú

Scríobh**ann** sé

Scríobh**ann** sí

Scríobh**aimid**

Scríobh**ann** sibh

Scríobh**ann** siad

An scríobh**ann**?

✓ Scríobh**ann**

✗ **Ní** scríobh**ann**

Aimsir Fháistineach	Modh Coinníollach
Scríobh**faidh** mé	Scríobh**fainn**
Scríobh**faidh** tú	Scríobh**fá**
Scríobh**faidh** sé	Scríobh**fadh** sé
Scríobh**faidh** sí	Scríobh**fadh** sí
Scríobh**faimid**	Scríobh**faimis**
Scríobh**faidh** sibh	Scríobh**fadh** sibh
Scríobh**faidh** siad	Scríobh**faidís**

An scríobh**faidh**?	**An** scríobh**fadh**?
✓ Scríobh**faidh**	✓ Scríobh**fadh**
✗ **Ní** scríobh**faidh**	✗ **Ní** scríobh**fadh**

Siúil
to walk

Aimsir Chaite	Aimsir Láithreach
Shiúil mé	Siúl**aim**
Shiúil tú	Siúl**ann** tú
Shiúil sé	Siúl**ann** sé
Shiúil sí	Siúl**ann** sí
Shiúl**amar**	Siúl**aimid**
Shiúil sibh	Siúl**ann sibh**
Shiúil siad	Siúl**ann** siad
Ar shiúil?	**An** siúl**ann**?
✓ **Sh**iúil	✓ Siúl**ann**
✗ **Níor sh**iúil	✗ **Ní sh**iúl**ann**

41

Aimsir Fháistineach	**Modh Coinníollach**
Siúl**faidh** mé	**Shiúlfainn**
Siúl**faidh** tú	**Shiúlfá**
Siúl**faidh** sé	**Shiúlfadh** sé
Siúl**faidh** sí	**Shiúlfadh** sí
Siúl**faimid**	**Shiúlfaimis**
Siúl**faidh** sibh	**Shiúlfadh** sibh
Siúl**faidh** siad	**Shiúlfaidís**
An siúl**faidh**?	**An** siúl**fadh**?
✓ Siúl**faidh**	✓ **Shiúlfadh**
✗ **Ní** shiúl**faidh**	✗ **Ní shiúlfadh**

Tóg
to take / to build

Aimsir Chaite	Aimsir Láithreach
Thóg mé	**Tóg**aim
Thóg tú	Tóg**ann** tú
Thóg sé	Tóg**ann** sé
Thóg sí	Tóg**ann** sí
Thóg**amar**	**Tóg**aimid
Thóg sibh	Tóg**ann** sibh
Thóg siad	Tóg**ann** siad
Ar thóg?	**An dtóg**ann?
✓ **Th**óg	✓ Tóg**ann**
✗ **Níor th**óg	✗ **Ní th**ógann

Aimsir Fháistineach	Modh Coinníollach
Tóg**faidh** mé	**Th**óg**fainn**
Tóg**faidh** tú	**Th**óg**fá**
Tóg**faidh** sé	**Th**óg**fadh** sé
Tóg**faidh** sí	**Th**óg**fadh** sí
Tóg**faimid**	**Th**óg**faimis**
Tóg**faidh** sibh	**Th**óg**fadh** sibh
Tóg**faidh** siad	**Th**óg**faidís**
An dtóg**faidh**?	**An d**tóg**fadh**?
✓ Tóg**faidh**	✓ **Th**óg**fadh**
✗ **Ní th**óg**faidh**	✗ **Ní th**óg**fadh**

Two-syllable verbs

Aistrigh
to change

Aimsir Chaite	Aimsir Láithreach
D'aistrigh mé	Aistr**ím**
D'aistrigh tú	Aistr**íonn** tú
D'aistrigh sé	Aistr**íonn** sé
D'aistrigh sí	Aistr**íonn** sí
D'aistr**íomar**	Aistr**ímid**
D'aistrigh sibh	Aistr**íonn** sibh
D'aistrigh siad	Aistr**íonn** siad
Ar aistrigh?	**An aistríonn**?
✓ **D'**aistrigh	✓ Aistr**íonn**
✗ **Níor** aistrigh	✗ **Ní** aistríonn

45

Aimsir Fháistineach	Modh Coinníollach
Aistr**eoidh** mé	**D'**aistr**eoinn**
Aistr**eoidh** tú	**D'**aistr**eofá**
Aistr**eoidh** sé	**D'**aistr**eodh** sé
Aistr**eoidh** sí	**D'**aistr**eodh** sí
Aistr**eoimid**	**D'**aistr**eoimis**
Aistr**eoidh** sibh	**D'**aistr**eodh** sibh
Aistr**eoidh** siad	**D'**aistr**eoidís**

An aistr**eoidh**?	**An** aistr**eodh**?
✓ Aistr**eoidh**	✓ **D'**aistr**eodh**
✗ **Ní** aistr**eoidh**	✗ **Ní** aistr**eodh**

Bailigh
to collect

slender

Aimsir Chaite

Bhailigh mé

Bhailigh tú

Bhailigh sé

Bhailigh sí

Bhailíomar

Bhailigh sibh

Bhailigh siad

Ar bhailigh?

✓ Bhailigh

✗ **Níor** bhailigh

Aimsir Láithreach

Bailím

Bailíonn tú

Bailíonn sé

Bailíonn sí

Baillímid

Bailíonn sibh

Bailíonn siad

An mbailíonn?

✓ Bailíonn

✗ **Ní** bhailíonn

Aimsir Fháistineach	Modh Coinníollach
Baileoidh mé	Bhaileoinn
Baileoidh tú	Bhaileofá
Baileoidh sé	Bhaileodh sé
Baileoidh sí	Bhaileodh sí
Baileoimid	Bhaileoimis
Baileoidh sibh	Bhaileodh sibh
Baileoidh siad	Bhaileoidís

An mbaileoidh?	An bhaileodh?
✓ Baileoidh	✓ Bhaileodh
✗ Ní bhaileoidh	✗ Ní bhaileodh

Ceannaigh
to buy

Aimsir Chaite	Aimsir Láithreach
Cheannaigh mé	Ceann**aím**
Cheannaigh tú	Ceann**aíonn** tú
Cheannaigh sé	Ceann**aíonn** sé
Cheannaigh sí	Ceann**aíonn** sí
Cheann**aíomar**	Ceann**aímid**
Cheannaigh sibh	Ceann**aíonn** sibh
Cheannaigh siad	Ceann**aíonn** siad

Ar cheannaigh?	**An gc**eann**aíonn**?
✓ **Ch**eannaigh	✓ Ceann**aíonn**
✗ **Níor ch**eannaigh	✗ **Ní ch**eann**aíonn**

Aimsir Fháistineach	Modh Coinníollach
Ceann**óidh** mé	**Cheannóinn**
Ceann**óidh** tú	**Cheannófá**
Ceann**óidh** sé	**Cheannódh** sé
Ceann**óidh** sí	**Cheannódh** sí
Ceann**óimid**	**Cheannóimis**
Ceann**óidh** sibh	**Cheannódh** sibh
Ceann**óidh** siad	**Cheannóidís**

An gceann**óidh**?	**An gceannódh**?
✓ Ceann**óidh**	✓ **Cheannódh**
✗ **Ní ch**eann**óidh**	✗ **Ní cheannódh**

Ceangail
to tie

Aimsir Chaite	Aimsir Láithreach
Cheangail mé	Ceang**laím**
Cheangail tú	Ceang**laíonn** tú
Cheangail sé	Ceang**laíonn** sé
Cheangail sí	Ceang**laíonn** sí
Cheang**laíomar**	Ceang**laímid**
Cheangail sibh	Ceang**laíonn** sibh
Cheangail siad	Ceang**laíonn** siad

Ar cheangail?	**An gc**eang**laíonn**?
✓ **Ch**eangail	✓ Ceang**laíonn**
✗ **Níor ch**eagail	✗ **Ní ch**eang**laíonn**

Aimsir Fháistineach	Modh Coinníollach
Ceanglóidh mé	Cheanglóinn
Ceanglóidh tú	Cheanglófá
Ceanglóidh sé	Cheanglódh sé
Ceanglóidh sí	Cheanglóidh sí
Ceanglóimid	Cheanglóimis
Ceanglóidh sibh	Cheanglóidh sibh
Ceanglóidh siad	Cheanglóidís
An gceanglóidh?	**An gceanglódh?**
✓ Ceanglóidh	✓ Cheanglóidh
✗ **Ní cheanglóidh**	✗ **Ní cheanglódh**

Críochnaigh
to finish

Aimsir Chaite	Aimsir Láithreach
Chríochn**aigh** mé	Críochn**aím**
Chríochn**aigh** tú	Críochn**aíonn** tú
Chríochn**aigh** sé	Críochn**aíonn** sé
Chríochn**aigh** sí	Críochn**aíonn** sí
Chríochn**aíomar**	Críochn**aímid**
Chríochn**aigh** sibh	Críochn**aíonn** sibh
Chríochn**aigh** siad	Críochn**aíonn** siad

Ar chríochnaigh?	**An g**críochn**aíonn**?
✓ **Chr**íochnaigh	✓ Críochn**aíonn**
✗ **Níor ch**ríochnaigh	✗ **Ní ch**ríochn**aíonn**

Aimsir Fháistineach	Modh Coinníollach
Críochnóidh mé	Chríochnóinn
Críochnóidh tú	Chríochnófá
Críochnóidh sé	Chríochnódh sé
Críochnóidh sí	Chríochnódh sí
Críochnóimid	Chríochnóimis
Críochnóidh sibh	Chríochnódh sibh
Críochnóidh siad	Chríochnóidís

An gcríochnóidh?	An gcríochnódh?
✓ Críochnóidh	✓ Chríochnódh
✗ Ní chríochnóidh	✗ Ní chríochnódh

Deisigh
to repair

Aimsir Chaite	Aimsir Láithreach
Dheisigh mé	Deis**ím**
Dheisigh tú	Deis**íonn** tú
Dheisigh sé	Deis**íonn** sé
Dheisigh sí	Deis**íonn** sí
Dheis**íomar**	Deis**ímid**
Dheisigh sibh	Deis**íonn** sibh
Dheisigh siad	Deis**íonn** siad
Ar dheisigh?	**An nd**eis**íonn**?
✓ **Dh**eisigh	✓ Deis**íonn**
✗ **Níor dh**eisigh	✗ **Ní dh**eis**íonn**

Aimsir Fháistineach	Modh Coinníollach
Deiseoidh mé	Dheiseoinn
Deiseoidh tú	Dheiseofá
Deiseoidh sé	Dheiseodh sé
Deiseoidh sí	Dheiseodh sí
Deiseoimid	Dheiseoimis
Deiseoidh sibh	Dheiseodh sibh
Deiseoidh siad	Dheiseoidís
An ndeiseoidh?	An ndeiseodh?
✓ Deiseoidh	✓ Dheiseodh
✗ Ní dheiseoidh	✗ Ní dheiseodh

Dúisigh

to wake

Aimsir Chaite	Aimsir Láithreach
Dhúisigh mé	Dúis**ím**
Dhúisigh tú	Dúis**íonn** tú
Dhúisigh sé	Dúis**íonn** sé
Dhúisigh sí	Dúis**íonn** sí
Dhúis**íomar**	Dúis**ímid**
Dhúisigh sibh	Dúis**íonn** sibh
Dhúisigh siad	Dúis**íonn** siad
Ar dhúisigh?	**An nd**úis**íonn**?
✓ **Dh**úisigh	✓ Dúis**íonn**
✗ **Níor dh**úisigh	✗ **Ní dh**úis**íonn**

Aimsir Fháistineach	Modh Coinníollach
Dúiseoidh mé	Dhúiseoinn
Dúiseoidh tú	Dhúiseofá
Dúiseoidh sé	Dhúiseodh sé
Dúiseoidh sí	Dhúiseodh sí
Dúiseoimid	Dhúiseoimis
Dúiseoidh sibh	Dhúiseodh sibh
Dúiseoidh siad	Dhúiseoidís

Aimsir Fháistineach	Modh Coinníollach
An ndúiseoidh?	An ndúiseodh?
✓ Dúiseoidh	✓ Dhúiseodh
✗ Ní dhúiseoidh	✗ Ní dhúiseodh

Éirigh

to rise

Aimsir Chaite	Aimsir Láithreach
D'éirigh mé	Éir**ím**
D'éirigh tú	Éir**íonn** tú
D'éirigh sé	Éir**íonn** sé
D'éirigh sí	Éir**íonn** sí
D'éir**íomar**	Éir**ímid**
D'éirigh sibh	Éir**íonn** sibh
D'éirigh siad	Éir**íonn** siad
Ar éirigh?	**An** éir**íonn**?
✓ **D'**éirigh	✓ Éir**íonn**
✗ **Níor** éirigh	✗ **Ní** éir**íonn**

Aimsir Fháistineach

Éireoidh mé

Éireoidh tú

Éireoidh sé

Éireoidh sí

Éireoimid

Éireoidh sibh

Éireoidh siad

An éireoidh?

✓ Éireoidh

✗ Ní éireoidh

Modh Coinníollach

D'éireoinn

D'éireofá

D'éireodh sé

D'éireodh sí

D'éireoimis

D'éireodh sibh

D'éireoidís

An éireodh?

✓ D'éireodh

✗ Ní éireodh

Foghlaim
to learn

Aimsir Chaite	Aimsir Láithreach
D'fhoghlaim mé	Foghlaim**ím**
D'fhoghlaim tú	Foghlaim**íonn** tú
D'fhoghlaim sé	Foghlaim**íonn** sé
D'fhoghlaim sí	Foghlaim**íonn** sí
D'fhoghlaim**íomar**	Foghlaim**ímid**
D'fhoghlaim sibh	Foghlaim**íonn** sibh
D'fhoghlaim siad	Foghlaim**íonn** siad

Ar fhoghlaim?	**An bh**foghlaim**íonn**?
✓ **D'fh**oghlaim	✓ Foghlaim**íonn**
✗ **Níor** fhoghlaim	✗ **Ní fh**oghlaim**íonn**

Foghlaim**eoidh** mé	**D'fhoghlaimeoinn**
Foghlaim**eoidh** tú	**D'fhoghlaimeofá**
Foghlaim**eoidh** sé	**D'fhoghlaimeodh** sé
Foghlaim**eoidh** sí	**D'fhoghlaimeodh** sí
Foghlaim**eoimid**	**D'fhoghlaimeoimis**
Foghlaim**eoidh** sibh	**D'fhoghlaimeodh** sibh
Foghlaim**eoidh** siad	**D'fhoghlaimeoidís**

An bhfoghlaim**eoidh**?	**An bhf**oghlaim**eodh**?
✓ Foghlaim**eoidh**	✓ **D'fhoghlaimeodh**
✗ **Ní fh**oghlaim**eoidh**	✗ **Ní fh**oghlaim**eodh**

Imigh

to leave

Aimsir Chaite	Aimsir Láithreach
D'imigh mé	Im**ím**
D'imigh tú	Im**íonn** tú
D'imigh sé	Im**íonn** sé
D'imigh sí	Im**íonn** sí
D'im**íomar**	Im**ímid**
D'imigh sibh	Im**íonn** sibh
D'imigh siad	Im**íonn** siad

Ar imigh?	**An** imíonn?
✓ **D'**imigh	✓ Im**íonn**
✗ **Níor** imigh	✗ **Ní** imíonn

63

Aimsir Fháistineach	Modh Coinníollach
Imeoidh mé	**D'**imeoinn
Imeoidh tú	**D'**imeofá
Imeoidh sé	**D'**imeodh sé
Imeoidh sí	**D'**imeodh sí
Imeoimid	**D'**imeoimis
Imeoidh sibh	**D'**imeodh sibh
Imeoidh siad	**D'**imeoidís
An imeoidh?	**An** imeodh?
✓ **Im**eoidh	✓ **D'**imeodh
✗ **Ní** imeoidh	✗ **Ní** imeodh

Imir
to play

slender

Aimsir Chaite

D'imir mé

D'imir tú

D'imir sé

D'imir sí

D'im**ríomar**

D'imir sibh

D'imir siad

Ar imir?

✓ **D'**imir

✗ **Níor** imir

Aimsir Láithreach

Imr**ím**

Imr**íonn** tú

Imr**íonn** sé

Imr**íonn** sí

Imr**ímid**

Imr**íonn** sibh

Imr**íonn** siad

An imr**íonn**?

✓ Imr**íonn**

✗ **Ní** imr**íonn**

Aimsir Fháistineach	Modh Coinníollach
Imr**eoidh** mé	**D'**imr**eoinn**
Imr**eoidh** tú	**D'**imr**eofá**
Imr**eoidh** sé	**D'**imr**eodh** sé
Imr**eoidh** sí	**D'**imr**eodh** sí
Imr**eoimid**	**D'**imr**eoimis**
Imr**eoidh** sibh	**D'**imr**eodh** sibh
Imr**eoidh** siad	**D'**imr**eoidís**
An imr**eoidh**?	**An** imr**eodh**?
✓ Imr**eoidh**	✓ **D'**imr**eodh**
✗ **Ní** imr**eoidh**	✗ **Ní** imr**eodh**

Inis (do)
to tell (to)

Aimsir Chaite	Aimsir Láithreach
D'inis mé	In**sím**
D'inis tú	In**síonn** tú
D'inis sé	In**síonn** sé
D'inis sí	In**síonn** sí
D'in**síomar**	In**símid**
D'inis sibh	In**síonn** sibh
D'inis siad	In**síonn** siad

Ar inis?	**An** in**síonn**?
✓ **D'**inis	✓ In**síonn**
✗ **Níor** inis	✗ **Ní** in**síonn**

Inis dom!

do

dom	dúinn
duit	díobh
dó/di	dóibh

Aimsir Fháistineach

Ins**eoidh** mé

Ins**eoidh** tú

Ins**eoidh** sé

Ins**eoidh** sí

Ins**eoimid**

Ins**eoidh** sibh

Ins**eoidh** siad

An ins**eoidh**?

✓ Ins**eoidh**

✗ **Ní** ins**eoidh**

Modh Coinníollach

D'inseoinn

D'inseofá

D'inseodh sé

D'inseodh sí

D'inseoimis

D'inseodh sibh

D'inseoidís

An ins**eodh**?

✓ **D'**ins**eodh**

✗ **Ní** ins**eodh**

Oscail
to open

Aimsir Chaite

D'oscail mé

D'oscail tú

D'oscail sé

D'oscail sí

D'osclaíomar

D'oscail sibh

D'oscail siad

Ar oscail?

✓ **D'oscail**

✗ **Níor** oscail

Aimsir Láithreach

Oscl**aím**

Oscl**aíonn** tú

Oscl**aíonn** sé

Oscl**aíonn** sí

Oscl**aímid**

Oscl**aíonn** sibh

Oscl**aíonn** siad

An oscl**aíonn**?

✓ Oscl**aíonn**

✗ **Ní** oscl**aíonn**

Aimsir Fháistineach

Osclóidh mé

Osclóidh tú

Osclóidh sé

Osclóidh sí

Osclóimid

Osclóidh sibh

Osclóidh siad

An osclóidh?

✓ Osclóidh

✗ Ní osclóidh

Modh Coinníollach

D'osclóinn

D'osclófá

D'osclódh sé

D'osclódh sí

D'osclóimis

D'osclódh sibh

D'osclóidís

An osclódh?

✓ D'osclódh

✗ Ní osclódh

Taispeáin

to show

Aimsir Chaite

Thaispeáin mé

Thaispeáin tú

Thaispeáin sé

Thaispeáin sí

Thaispe**ánamar**

Thaispeáin sibh

Thaispeáin siad

Ar thaispeáin?

✓ **Th**aispeáin

✗ **Níor th**aispeáin

Aimsir Láithreach

Taispe**ánaim**

Taispe**ánann** tú

Taispe**ánann** sé

Taispe**ánann** sí

Taispe**ánaimid**

Taispe**ánann** sibh

Taispe**ánann** siad

An dtaispe**ánann**?

✓ Taispe**ánann**

✗ **Ní th**aispe**ánann**

Aimsir Fháistineach

Taispeán**faidh** mé

Taispeán**faidh** tú

Taispeán**faidh** sé

Taispeán**faidh** sí

Taispeán**faimid**

Taispeán**faidh** sibh

Taispeán**faidh** siad

An dtaispeán**faidh**?

✓ Taispeán**faidh**

✗ **Ní th**aispeán**faidh**

Modh Coinníollach

Thaispeán**fainn**

Thaispeán**fá**

Thaispeán**fadh** sé

Thaispeán**fadh** sí

Thaispeán**faimis**

Thaispeán**fadh** sibh

Thaispeán**faidís**

An dtaispeán**fadh**?

✓ **Th**aispeán**fadh**

✗ **Ní th**aispeán**fadh**

Tarraing
to pull / to draw

slender

Aimsir Chaite

Tharraing mé

Tharraing tú

Tharraing sé

Tharraing sí

Tharraing**íomar**

Tharraing sibh

Tharraing siad

Ar tharraing?

✓ **Th**arraing

✗ **Níor th**arraing

Aimsir Láithreach

Tarraing**ím**

Tarraing**íonn** tú

Tarraing**íonn** sé

Tarraing**íonn** sí

Tarraing**ímid**

Tarraing**íonn** sibh

Tarraing**íonn** siad

An dtarraing**íonn**?

✓ Tarraing**íonn**

✗ **Ní th**arraing**íonn**

Aimsir Fháistineach	Modh Coinníollach
Tarraing**eoidh** mé	**Th**arraing**eoinn**
Tarraing**eoidh** tú	**Th**arraing**eofá**
Tarraing**eoidh** sé	**Th**arraing**eodh** sé
Tarraing**eoidh** sí	**Th**arraing**eodh** sí
Tarraing**eoimid**	**Th**arraing**eoimis**
Tarraing**eoidh** sibh	**Th**arraing**eodh** sibh
Tarraing**eoidh** siad	**Th**arraing**eoidís**

An dtarraing**eoidh**?	**An dt**arraing**eodh**?
✓ Tarraing**eoidh**	✓ **Th**arraing**eodh**
✗ **Ní th**arraing**eoidh**	✗ **Ní th**arraing**eodh**

Tosaigh
to start

Aimsir Chaite	Aimsir Láithreach
Thosaigh mé	Tos**aím**
Thosaigh tú	Tos**aíonn** tú
Thosaigh sé	Tos**aíonn** sé
Thosaigh sí	Tos**aíonn** sí
Thosaíomar	Tos**aímid**
Thosaigh sibh	Tos**aíonn** sibh
Thosaigh siad	Tos**aíonn** siad
Ar thosaigh?	**An dt**osaíonn?
✓ **Th**osaigh	✓ Tos**aíonn**
✗ **Níor th**osaigh	✗ **Ní th**osaíonn

Aimsir Fháistineach	Modh Coinníollach
Tos**óidh** mé	**Thosóinn**
Tos**óidh** tú	**Thosófá**
Tos**óidh** sé	**Thosódh** sé
Tos**óidh** sí	**Thosódh** sí
Tos**óimid**	**Thosóimis**
Tos**óidh** sibh	**Thosódh** sibh
Tos**óidh** siad	**Thosóidís**
An dtos**óidh**?	**An dt**os**ódh**?
✓ Tos**óidh**	✓ **Thosódh**
✗ **Ní thosóidh**	✗ **Ní thosódh**

Ullmhaigh

to prepare

Aimsir Chaite

D'ullmhaigh mé

D'ullmhaigh tú

D'ullmhaigh sé

D'ullmhaigh sí

D'ullmhaíomar

D'ullmhaigh sibh

D'ullmhaigh siad

Ar ullmhaigh?

✓ D'ullmhaigh

✗ Níor ullmhaigh

Aimsir Láithreach

Ullmhaím

Ullmhaíonn tú

Ullmhaíonn sé

Ullmhaíonn sí

Ullmhaímid

Ullmhaíonn sibh

Ullmhaíonn siad

An ullmhaíonn?

✓ Ullmhaíonn

✗ Ní ullmhaíonn

Aimsir Fháistineach	Modh Coinníollach
Ullmh**óidh** mé	**D'**ullmh**óinn**
Ullmh**óidh** tú	**D'**ullmh**ófá**
Ullmh**óidh** sé	**D'**ullmh**ódh** sé
Ullmh**óidh** sí	**D'**ullmh**ódh** sí
Ullmh**óimid**	**D'**ullmh**óimis**
Ullmh**óidh** sibh	**D'**ullmh**ódh** sibh
Ullmh**óidh** siad	**D'**ullmh**óidís**

An ullmh**óidh**?	**An** ullmh**ódh**?
✓ Ullmh**óidh**	✓ **D'**ullmh**ódh**
✗ **Ní** ullmh**óidh**	✗ **Ní** ullmh**ódh**

Irregular verbs

Abair (le)
to say (to someone)

Aimsir Chaite	Aimsir Láithreach
Dúirt mé (le)	Deir**im** (le)
Dúirt tú	Deir tú
Dúirt sé	Deir sé
Dúirt sí	Deir sí
Dúramar	Deir**imid**
Dúirt sibh	Deir sibh
Dúirt siad	Deir siad

An ndúirt?	**An n**deir?
✓ **Dúirt**	✓ **Deir**
✗ **Ní d**úirt	✗ **Ní deir**

le

liom	linn
leat	libh
leis/léi	leo

Aimsir Fháistineach

Déarfaidh mé (le)

Déarfaidh tú

Déarfaidh sé

Déarfaidh sí

Déarfaimid

Déarfaidh sibh

Déarfaidh siad

An ndéarfaidh?

✓ Déarfaidh

✗ **Ní dhéarfaidh**

Modh Coinníollach

Déarfainn

Déarfá

Déarfadh sé

Déarfadh sí

Déarfaimis

Déarfadh sibh

Déarfaidís

An ndéarfadh?

✓ Déarfadh

✗ **Ní** déarfadh

Beir

to catch / to grab / to hold

Aimsir Chaite

Rug mé (ar)

Rug tú

Rug sé

Rug sí

Rugamar

Rug sibh

Rug siad

Ar rug?

✓ Rug

✗ **Níor** rug

Aimsir Láithreach

Beir**im** (ar)

Beir**eann** tú

Beir**eann** sé

Beir**eann** sí

Beir**imid**

Beir**eann** sibh

Beir**eann** siad

An mbeir**eann**?

✓ Beir**eann**

✗ **Ní bh**eir**eann**

Aimsir Fháistineach	Modh Coinníollach
Béar**faidh** mé (ar)	**Bhéarfainn** (ar)
Béar**faidh** tú	**Bhéarfá**
Béar**faidh** sé	**Bhéarfadh** sé
Béar**faidh** sí	**Bhéarfadh** sí
Béar**faimid**	**Bhéarfaimis**
Béar**faidh** sibh	**Bhéarfadh** sibh
Béar**faidh** siad	**Bhéarfaidís**

An mbéar**faidh**?	**An mb**éar**fadh**?
✓ Béar**faidh**	✓ **Bhéarfadh**
✗ **Ní bh**éar**faidh**	✗ **Ní bh**éar**fadh**

Bí
to be

Tá to be right now

Aimsir Chaite	Aimsir Láithreach
Bhí mé	**Bí**m
Bhí tú	**Bí**onn tú
Bhí sé	**Bí**onn sé
Bhí sí	**Bí**onn sí
Bhíomar	**Bí**mid
Bhí sibh	**Bí**onn sibh
Bhí siad	**Bí**onn siad
An raibh?	**An mbíonn**?
✓ **Bhí**	✓ **Bíonn**
✗ **Ní** raibh	✗ **Ní bhíonn**

Tá mé/Táim	Tá sibh
Tá tú	Tá siad
Tá sé/sí	
Táimid	

An bhfuil?
- ✓ Tá
- ✗ Níl

To be or not to be...

Aimsir Fháistineach

Beidh mé

Beidh tú

Beidh sé

Beidh sí

Bei**mid**

Beidh sibh

Beidh siad

An mbeidh?

- ✓ Beidh
- ✗ **Ní bh**eidh

Modh Coinníollach

Bhe**inn**

Bhe**ifeá**

Bhe**adh** sé

Bhe**adh** sí

Bhe**imis**

Bhe**adh** sibh

Bhe**idís**

An mbeadh?

- ✓ Bhe**adh**
- ✗ **Ní** bhe**adh**

Clois
to hear

|

Aimsir Chaite

Chuala mé

Chuala tú

Chuala sé

Chuala sí

Chualamar

Chuala sibh

Chuala siad

Ar chuala?

✓ **Ch**uala

✗ **Níor ch**uala

Aimsir Láithreach

Clois**im**

Clois**eann** tú

Clois**eann** sé

Clois**eann** sí

Clois**imid**

Clois**eann** sibh

Clois**eann** siad

An gclois**eann**?

✓ Clois**eann**

✗ **Ní ch**loiseann

Aimsir Fháistineach	Modh Coinníollach
Clois**fidh** mé	**Ch**lois**finn**
Clois**fidh** tú	**Ch**lois**feá**
Clois**fidh** sé	**Ch**lois**feadh** sé
Clois**fidh** sí	**Ch**lois**feadh** sí
Clois**fimid**	**Ch**lois**fimis**
Clois**fidh** sibh	**Ch**lois**feadh** sibh
Clois**fidh** siad	**Ch**lois**fidís**
An gclois**fidh**?	**An g**clois**feadh**?
✓ Clois**fidh**	✓ **Ch**lois**feadh**
✗ **Ní ch**lois**fidh**	✗ **Ní ch**lois**feadh**

Déan

to do / to make

Aimsir Chaite

Rinne mé

Rinne tú

Rinne sé

Rinne sí

Rinn**eamar**

Rinne sibh

Rinne siad

An ndearna?

✓ Rinne

✗ **Ní dh**earna mé

Aimsir Láithreach

Déan**aim**

Déan**ann** tú

Déan**ann** sé

Déan**ann** sí

Déan**aimid**

Déan**ann** sibh

Déan**ann** siad

An ndéan**ann**?

✓ Déan**ann**

✗ **Ní dh**éan**ann**

Aimsir Fháistineach

Déan**faidh** mé

Déan**faidh** tú

Déan**faidh** sé

Déan**faidh** sí

Déan**faimid**

Déan**faidh** sibh

Déan**faidh** siad

An ndéan**faidh**?

✓ Déan**faidh**

✗ **Ní dh**éan**faidh**

Modh Coinníollach

Dhéann**fainn**

Dhéan**fá**

Dhéan**fadh** sé

Dhéan**fadh** sí

Dhéan**faimis**

Dhéan**fadh** sibh

Dhéan**faidís**

An ndéan**fadh**?

✓ **Dh**éan**fadh**

✗ **Ní dh**éan**fadh**

Faigh
to get

Fuair mé

Fuair tú

Fuair sé

Fuair sí

Fuair**eamar**

Fuair sibh

Fuair siad

An bhfuair?

✓ Fuair

✗ **Ní bh**fuair

Faigh**im**

Faigh**eann** tú

Faigh**eann** sé

Faigh**eann** sí

Faigh**imid**

Faigh**eann** sibh

Faigh**eann** siad

An bhfaigheann?

✓ Faigh**eann**

✗ **Ní fh**aigheann

Aimsir Fháistineach	Modh Coinníollach
Gheobhaidh mé	**Gheobhainn**
Gheobhaidh tú	**Gheobhfá**
Gheobhaidh sé	**Gheobhadh** sé
Gheobhaidh sí	**Gheobhadh** sí
Gheobhaimid	**Gheobhaimis**
Gheobhaidh sibh	**Gheobhadh** sibh
Gheobhaidh siad	**Gheobhaidís**
An bhfaigh**idh**?	**An bh**faigh**eadh**?
✓ Gheobh**aidh**	✓ Gheobh**adh**
✗ **Ní bh**faigh**idh**	✗ **Ní bh**faigh**eadh**

Feic

to see

Chonaic mé

Chonaic tú

Chonaic sé

Chonaic sí

Chonaic**eamar**

Chonaic sibh

Chonaic siad

An bhfaca tú?

✓ **Ch**onaic

✗ **Ní fh**aca

Feic**im**

Feic**eann** tú

Feic**eann** sé

Feic**eann** sí

Feic**imid**

Feic**eann** sibh

Feic**eann** siad

An bhfeic**eann**?

✓ Feic**eann**

✗ **Ní fh**eic**eann**

Aimsir Fháistineach	Modh Coinníollach
Feicfidh mé	D'fheicfinn
Feicfidh tú	D'fheicfeá
Feicfidh sé	D'fheicfeadh sé
Feicfidh sí	D'fheicfeadh sí
Feicfimid	D'fheicfimis
Feicfidh sibh	D'fheicfeadh sibh
Feicfidh siad	D'fheicfidís

An bhfeicfidh?

✓ Feicfidh

✗ **Ní fh**eic**fidh**

An bhfeicfeadh?

✓ **D'fheicfeadh**

✗ **Ní fh**eic**feadh**

Ith

to eat

Aimsir Chaite	Aimsir Láithreach
D'ith mé	Ith**im**
D'ith tú	Ith**eann** tú
D'ith sé	Ith**eann** sé
D'ith sí	Ith**eann** sí
D'ith**eamar**	Ith**imid**
D'ith sibh	Ith**eann** sibh
D'ith siad	Ith**eann** siad
Ar ith?	**An** ith**eann**?
✓ **D'**ith	✓ Ith**eann**
✗ **Níor** ith	✗ **Ní** ith**eann**

Aimsir Fháistineach	Modh Coinníollach
Íosfaidh mé	D'íosfainn
Íosfaidh tú	D'íosfá
Íosfaidh sé	D'íosfadh sé
Íosfaidh sí	D'íosfadh sí
Íosfaimid	D'íosfaimis
Íosfaidh sibh	D'íosfadh sibh
Íosfaidh siad	D'íosfaidís
An Íos**faidh**?	**An** íos**fadh**?
✓ Íos**faidh**	✓ **D'**íos**fadh**
✗ **Ní** Íos**faidh**	✗ **Ní** íos**fadh**

Tabhair
to give

Aimsir Chaite

Thug mé

Thug tú

Thug sé

Thug sí

Thug**amar**

Thug sibh

Thug siad

Ar thug?

✓ **Th**ug

✗ **Níor th**ug

Aimsir Láithreach

Tug**aim**

Tug**ann** tú

Tug**ann** sé

Tug**ann** sí

Tug**aimid**

Tug**ann** sibh

Tug**ann** siad

An dtug**ann**?

✓ Tug**ann**

✗ **Ní th**ug**ann**

<table>
<tr><td>

Aimsir Fháistineach

Tabhar**faidh** mé

Tabhar**faidh** tú

Tabhar**faidh** sé

Tabhar**faidh** sí

Tabhar**faimid**

Tabhar**faidh** sibh

Tabhar**faidh** siad

An dtabhar**faidh**?

✓ Tabhar**faidh**

✗ **Ní th**abhar**faidh**

</td><td>

Modh Coinníollach

Thabhar**fainn**

Thabhar**fá**

Thabhar**fadh** sé

Thabhar**fadh** sí

Thabhar**faimis**

Thabhar**fadh** sibh

Thabhar**faidís**

An dtabhar**fadh**?

✓ **Th**abhar**fadh**

✗ **Ní th**abhar**fadh**

</td></tr>
</table>

Tar

to come

Aimsir Chaite	Aimsir Láithreach
Tháinig mé	Tag**aim**
Tháinig tú	Tag**ann** tú
Tháinig sé	Tag**ann** sé
Tháinig sí	Tag**ann** sí
Thángamar	Tag**aimid**
Tháinig sibh	Tag**ann** sibh
Tháinig siad	Tag**ann** siad
Ar tháinig?	An dtag**ann**?
✓ **Th**áinig	✓ Tag**ann**
✗ **Níor th**áinig	✗ **Ní th**agann

Aimsir Fháistineach	Modh Coinníollach
Tiocfaidh mé	Thiocfainn
Tiocfaidh tú	Thiocfá
Tiocfaidh sé	Thiocfadh sé
Tiocfaidh sí	Thiocfadh sí
Tiocfaimid	Thiocfaimis
Tiocfaidh sibh	Thiocfadh sibh
Tiocfaidh siad	Thiocfaidís

An dtiocfaidh?

✓ Tiocfaidh

✗ **Ní thiocfaidh**

An dtiocfadh?

✓ **Thiocfadh**

✗ **Ní thiocfadh**

Téigh
to go

Aimsir Chaite

Chuaigh mé

Chuaigh tú

Chuaigh sé

Chuaigh sí

Chuamar

Chuaigh sibh

Chuaigh siad

An ndeachaigh?

✓ **Ch**uaigh

✗ **Ní nd**eachaigh

Aimsir Láithreach

Téim

Téann tú

Téann sé

Téann sí

Téimid

Téann sibh

Téann siad

An dtéann?

✓ Té**ann**

✗ **Ní** thé**ann**

TÉIGH

Aimsir Fháistineach	Modh Coinníollach
Rach**aidh** mé	Rach**ainn**
Rach**aidh** tú	Rach**fá**
Rach**aidh** sé	Rach**adh** sé
Rach**aidh** sí	Rach**adh** sí
Rach**aimid**	Rach**aimis**
Rach**aidh** sibh	Rach**adh** sibh
Rach**aidh** siad	Rach**aidís**

An rach**aidh**?	**An** rach**adh**?
✓ Rach**aidh**	✓ Rach**adh**
✗ **Ní** rach**aidh**	✗ **Ní** rach**adh**

Briathra Eile

Many verbs end in the same way

Bris – Break (p.3)
Béic – Shout
Buail – Hit / Meet
Creid – Believe
Goid – Steal
Múin – Teach
Tuig – Understand

Dóigh – Burn (p.15)
Clóigh – Print
Reoigh – Freeze

Dún – Close (p.17)
Cas – Turn
Cnag – Knock
Croch – Hang
Cum – Compose
Las – Light
Mol – Praise
Póg – Kiss

Fág – Leave (p.21)
Fás – Grow
Fiuch – Boil

Nigh – Wash (p.33)
Ligh – Lick
Luigh – Lie (down)
Suigh – Sit

Ól – Drink (p. 35)
Athdhíol – Resell
Athscríobh – Rewrite
Íoc – Pay

Rith – Run (p.37)
Tit – Fall

Scríobh – Write (p.39)
Sciob – Snatch
Scread – Scream
Stad – Stop
Spreag – Urge

Dúisigh – Wake (p.57)
Ceistigh – Question
Cuidigh – Help
Maisigh – Decorate
Mínigh – Explain

Éirigh – Rise (p.59)
Ainmnigh – Name
Impigh – Beg
Aimsigh – Locate

Foghlaim – Learn (p.61)
Codail – Sleep
Freastail – Attend
Taistil – Travel
Tuirling – Descend

Imir – Play (p.65)
Freagair – Answer
Iompair – Carry
Fógair – Announce

Oscail – Open (p.69)
Athmhúscail – Reawake
Cuimil – Rub
Eitil – Fly
Tochaill – Dig

Taispeáin – Show (p.71)
Adhlaic – Bury
Ceiliúir – Celebrate
Gearán – Complain
Tiomáin – Drive
Tíolaic – Present

Ullmhaigh (p.77)
Admhaigh – Admit
Aontaigh – Agree
Éalaigh – Escape
Ionsaigh – Attack
Iompaigh – Turn
Ordaigh – Order

Réamhfhocail

Prepositions

Adding **'an'** (the) changes the way we use prepositions.

Examples:

1. If you want to say **'the man <u>with the</u> hat'**:
   – **'le'** (with) and **'an'** (the) become **'leis an'** (with the) and so we say **'an fear leis an hata'**.

2. If you want to say, **'He is <u>in the</u> shop'**:
   – **'i'** (in) and **'an'** (the) become **'sa'** (in the), and so we say, **'Tá sé <u>sa</u> siopa'**.

i + an
  sa = in the (used before consonants)

in + an
  san = in the (used before vowels)

i + na
  sna = in the (plural)

ó + an
  ón = from the

le + an
  leis an = with the

le + na
  lena = with the (plural)

do + an
  don = to the / for the

Sampla
ar – *on*
orm – *on me*
ort – *on you*
air – *on him*
uirthi – *on her*
orainn – *on us*
oraibh – *on you all*
orthu – *on them*

Simple Prepositions

ag – *at*
agam
agat
aige
aici
againn
agaibh
acu

chuig – *towards*
chugam
chugat
chuige
chuici
chugainn
chugaibh
chucu

as – *out*
asam
asat
as
asti
asainn
asaibh
astu

le – *with*
liom
leat
leis
léi
linn
libh
leo

idir – *between*
idir mé
idir tú
idir é
idir í
eadrainn
eadraibh
eatarthu

de – *off*
díom
díot
de
di
dínn
díbh
díobh

um – *around*
umam
umat
uime
uimpi
umainn
umaibh
umpu

do – *for*
dom
duit
dó
di
dúinn
daoibh
dóibh

roimh – *before*
romham
romhat
roimhe
roimpi
romhainn
romhaibh
rompu

Simple Prepositions

ó – *from*	**thar** – *past*	**trí** – *through*
uaim	tharam	triom
uait	tharat	tríot
uaidh	thairis	tríd
uaithi	thairsti	tríthi
uainn	tharainn	trínn
uaibh	tharaibh	tríbh
uathu	tharstu	tríothu

faoi – *under*	**i** – *in*
fúm	ionam
fút	ionat
faoi	ann
fúithi	inti
fúinn	ionainn
fúibh	ionaibh
fúthu	iontu

Simple Prepositions

i ndiaidh – *after*
  i **mo dh**iaidh
  i **do dh**iaidh
  ina dhiaidh
  ina diaidh
  inár dhiaidh
  in **bhur nd**iaidh
  ina ndiaidh

os comhair – *opposite*
  os **mo ch**omhair
  os **do ch**omhair
  os **a ch**omhair
  os **a c**omhair
  os **ár gc**omhair
  os **bhur gc**omhair
  os **a gc**omhair

Compound Prepositions

in éadan – *against*
  i **m'**éadan
  i **d'**éadan
  ina éadan
  ina héadan
  inár n-éadan
  in **bhur n-**éadan
  ina n-éadan

os cionn – *above*
  os **mo ch**ionn
  os **do ch**ionn
  os **a ch**ionn
  os **a c**ionn
  os **ár gc**ionn
  os **bhur gc**ionn
  os **a gc**ionn

Cleachtadh na mBriathra

Ainm: _____

Aimsir Chaite	Aimsir Láithreach
_____	_____
_____	_____
_____	_____
_____	_____
_____	_____
_____	_____
_____	_____
_____ ?	_____ ?
✓ _____	✓ _____
✗ _____	✗ _____

Aimsir Fháistineach	Modh Coinníollach
_____	_____
_____	_____
_____	_____
_____	_____
_____	_____
_____	_____
_____	_____

_____ ?

✓ _____

✗ _____

_____ ?

✓ _____

✗ _____

Nótaí

Notes